First published 1982

Macdonald & Co
(Publishers) Ltd
Maxwell House
Worship Street
London EC2A 2EN

ISBN 0 356 07534 6 (cased)
ISBN 0 356 07528 1 (limp)

Made and printed by
Purnell and Sons
(Book Production) Ltd
Paulton England

Editor
Lis Edwards

Production
Rosemary Bishop

Picture research
Caroline Mitchell

Illustrators
Janet Blakeley/
N E Middleton
Richard Hook/Temple Art
(cover)
Elaine Lee/N E Middleton
Jim Robins/N E Middleton
Ken Stott/N E Middleton

Photographs
Aldus Archive 56 (B)
Courtesy of the Trustees of the British
Museum 14, 16
Giraudon 12(T)
Hever Castle 18
J. Allan Cash 29, 31(B)
Kunsthistorisches Museum, Vienna 23, 39, 41
The Mansell Collection 31(T), 32, 57(B)
Mary Evans Picture Library 28
MAS/El Escorial 44
MAS/Museo del Prado 17
Musee des Beaux Arts, Lausanne 13
Museum Boymans van Beuningen, Rotterdam 35
National Scheepvart Museum, Antwerp 52–3
Narodni Gallery, Prague 33
Reproduced by Gracious Permission of her Majesty
The Queen 8–9
Robert Harding Picture Library 21(R)
Scala/Bibliotheca Nationale, Firenze 56(T)
Scala/Palazzo Vecchio, Firenze 57(T)
Ullstein Bilderdienst 37
Victoria and Albert Museum 55
Woodmansterne Ltd. 27
Zefa 12(B), 21(L), 30

Everyday life in the sixteenth century

Haydn Middleton

Macdonald

The 16th century

Europe 400 years ago was a very different place from what it is today. England and Scotland each had its own royal family. There were no countries called Italy and Germany. The Netherlands belonged to the King of Spain, who was the most powerful Christian monarch. And, from the East, the mighty Turks were threatening to conquer the whole continent.

The everyday lives of European people were very different, too. Half the number of babies born died before their first birthdays. Anyone who lived to be 40 was thought very old. There were many plagues and diseases, and doctors could do little to cure them.

Women were kept under strict control by their fathers or husbands. They existed only to serve men, who were thought to be the masters. However, for much of this period England was ruled by a queen, Elizabeth I, who was one of the best-loved Tudor monarchs.

The rich and the poor lived in completely different worlds. The rich ate fantastic meals, wore gorgeous clothes and lived in beautiful homes. They had to pay few taxes, and could buy their children a good education.

But there were far more poor people than rich people. The poor often went hungry. In times of famine they even ate rats, tree-bark and roots. They wore simple, home-made clothes and rarely changed them. The homes of the poorest were tumbledown shacks, which they shared with their animals. They had very little money, but had to pay many taxes. Most poor people could not read or write, and they could not afford to send their children to school or university.

For most people at this time life was very hard. But they still found ways to enjoy themselves, and felt sure that God was watching over them. Life on Earth was not very important to them. Getting to Heaven was what really mattered.

Contents

Rulers of Europe

In the 16th century kings and queens liked to see themselves as gods. They ate, dressed and played in spectacular style. As they paraded from one magnificent palace to another, they struck awe and respect into their subjects. The power of royal families, like the Tudors in England, was immense. Parliaments had very little say in the running of kingdoms and empires.

One of the main jobs of a monarch was to provide law and order, so that his or her subjects could go about their daily business in safety. This meant ruthlessly crushing any rebellions. The usual price of disobedience was death. King Henry VIII of England even executed a close friend, Sir Thomas More, for failing to obey him.

It was often said that only a man could carry out all the duties of a monarch. Yet Queen Elizabeth I made herself one of the most highly-respected rulers in English history. The real problems arose when a child came to the throne. During the reign of the French boy-king Charles IX, power

▼ In June 1520, Henry VIII of England met Francis I of France at the Field of the Cloth of Gold, near Calais. Enormously expensive feasts and entertainments were laid on for the kings and their men. This painting shows Henry arriving (*bottom left*), and all the games and amusements that were on offer.

But Henry and Francis did not stay friends for long. Two years later they were at war with one another.

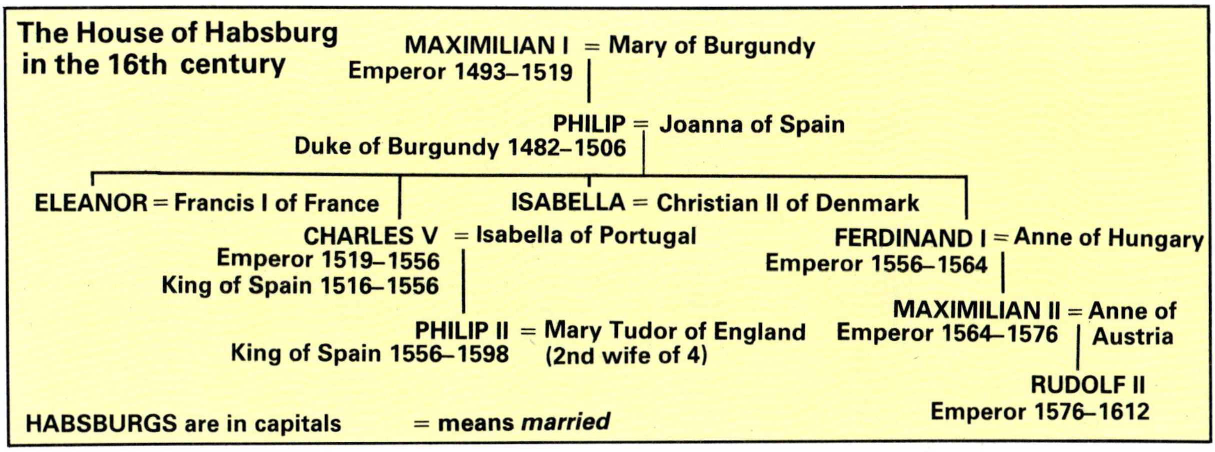

▲ The Habsburgs made a habit of marrying into other ruling families. In this way, they enlarged their empire.

was seized by a group of selfish nobles. Since the king was unable to keep the peace, France was almost destroyed by feuding.

Most monarchs tried to add to their lands through warfare and marriage. The Habsburg family of Austria built up the mightiest empire in Europe. From 1519 to 1555, Emperor Charles V ruled territories stretching from Spain to Hungary, and from Italy to the Netherlands. No wonder he saw himself as a god.

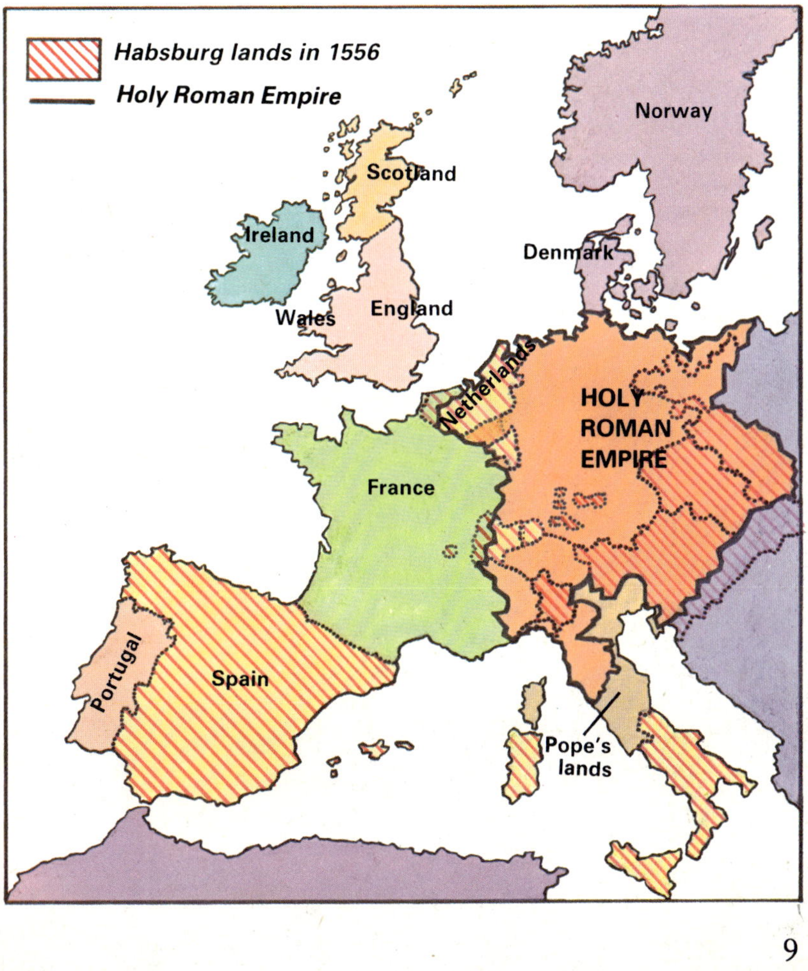

▼ This map shows western Europe in 1550. The Habsburgs seemed to be everywhere. A member of this family was usually elected to rule over the Holy Roman Empire too.

Europe and the world

Until the last years of the 15th century, Europeans knew very little about the rest of the world. They had made contact with distant empires in the East, but they had no idea that America even existed. By 1600, all this had changed completely. Curiosity alone did not lead to this 'Age of Discovery'. The rulers of Europe sent out their sailors for two purposes. The first was to search for a sea-route to the rich empires of Asia. The second was to turn any peoples they might meet into Christians.

The sailors of Portugal and Spain were the first to brave the oceans. In 1498 the Portuguese succeeded in reaching India, by sailing around the bottom of Africa. They went on to trade with India, the Spice Islands, China, and even Japan. The civilized inhabitants of most of these places looked down on the Portuguese adventurers. Very few of them wanted to take up European customs or Christianity.

The Spaniards tried to get to Asia by sailing westwards. When they reached America they believed that it was Asia. But as they explored the lands now called Mexico and Peru, they realized that they had discovered a 'New World', rich in gold and silver.

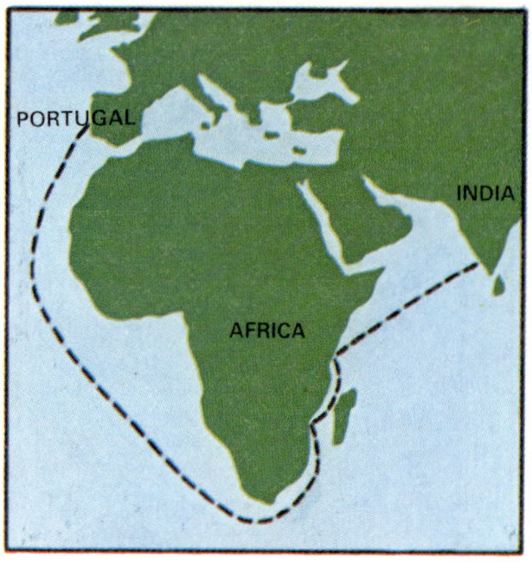

▲ The route of the first sea-expedition from Europe to India, led by Vasco da Gama. He left Portugal in mid-1497, and arrived in India almost a year later. This voyage blazed the trail for countless European merchants.

► A Spanish captain telling the Incas of Peru to become Christians or be killed.

The Incas had never seen horses before the Spaniards arrived in 1531. They thought that these strange beings might be gods. But the Spaniards behaved more like devils, when they destroyed the Inca Empire.

▶ This is a scene in 16th century Goa, from a book by an explorer about his travels. Goa was a large seaport in western India. In 1510, the Portuguese captured it and made it their chief port in Asia. From here, valuable spices like pepper, cinnamon and cloves were shipped back to Europe.

▼ In 1580 Queen Elizabeth I of England knighted Francis Drake on board his ship, the 'Golden Hind'. He had just returned from a three-year expedition round the world. Elizabeth called Drake her 'little master thief', because he brought back a massive haul of treasure, taken from Spanish ships.

The Spaniards brutally crushed the native Aztec and Inca civilizations, then set up their own vast American empire. At the same time, the Portuguese followed the Spaniards across the Atlantic, and set up their own huge colony in Brazil.

In 1580, King Philip II of Spain seized the Crown and Empire of Portugal. This made him the first ruler with territories stretching right round the world.

Religion and the people

In the 16th century men and women worried a lot about life after death. They relied on the Church to tell them how to live good lives on Earth, and hoped that God would reward them when they died. At the start of the century, all the countries of western Europe were Roman Catholic.

The Church was far more important than it is today. Church-bells announced the time for work or meals or rest. Church law-courts enforced Christian behaviour. Monasteries acted as schools, inns and hospitals. Bishops and cardinals were among a monarch's most trusted advisers.

But many priests, monks and bishops failed to set the people a good example. The Roman Catholic Church had become immensely rich. Too many clergymen cared more for wealth and pleasure than for their religious duties. Critics protested about the state of the Church, and suggested ways to improve it. The Catholic authorities took little notice. So these 'Protestants' began to set up their own churches.

One part of Europe after another took up Protestant beliefs. By the middle of the century, western Europe was split between Protestants and Catholics. Both believed that theirs was the true form of Christianity – and they were prepared to fight to the death to prove it. So Europe was torn apart by a series of savage wars, fought in God's name.

▲ Martin Luther, a German professor, started to complain about the Roman Catholic church in 1517. Eventually, he set up his own 'Protestant' or 'Lutheran' church.

◀ A 16th-century monastery and palace outside Madrid, called the Escorial. It was built on the orders of the Catholic King Philip II of Spain.

► On the eve of St Bartholomew's Day, 1572, Catholics in France turned on the Protestants and slaughtered them. This painting shows the horrifying scenes in Paris. In the centre, the Catholic King Charles IX is inspecting the cut-off head of a Protestant leader.

► Around 1550, Europe was a patchwork of different religions. Most people had to follow the religion of their rulers, or risk being savagely persecuted for their faith.

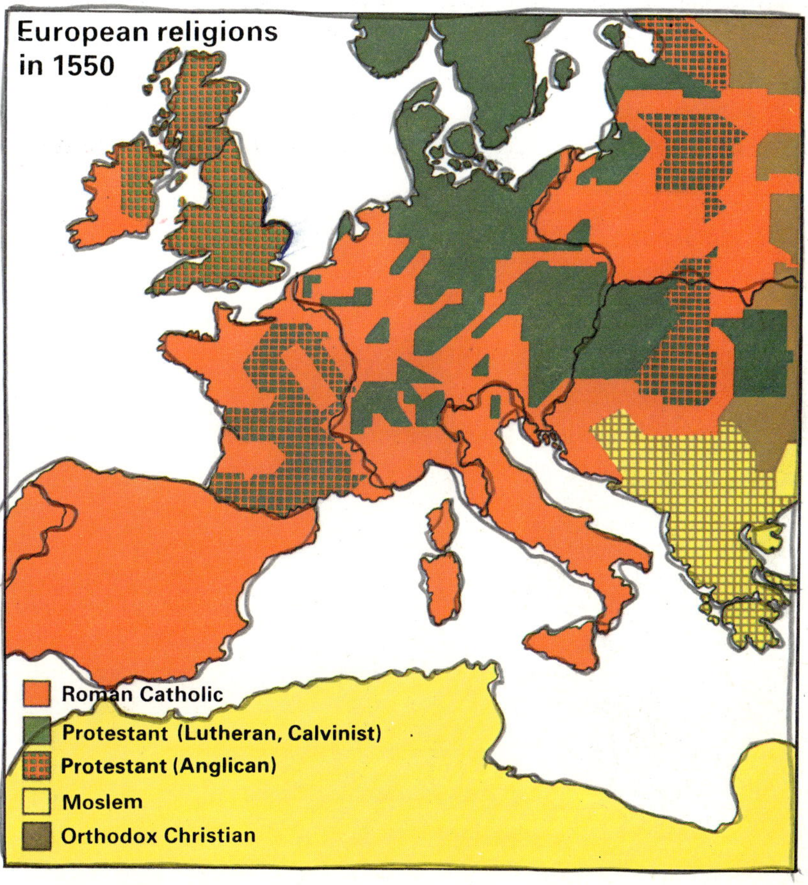

▼ A family studying the Bible. People often worshipped at home, as well as in church. Richer families even employed chaplains of their own.

The humble and the mighty

The rulers of Europe needed endless supplies of money. Fighting wars and building palaces were very expensive pastimes. Royal servants had to be paid to attend to the complicated business of government. Matters were made worse by a great and rapid increase in prices all over the continent. One way of raising more money was to demand higher taxes from the people.

In many parts of Europe, rich nobles and Church officials did not have to pay these taxes. Most of the burden fell on the peasants, who were already suffering terribly from the rise in the cost of living. These peasants not only paid taxes to their rulers; they also had to pay dues to their local lords, and tithes to their local clergy.

Now and then, peasants resisted the unfair demands made on them. It is surprising to us that they did not rebel more often. Today we believe that all people are equal, and should therefore be treated the same. But people in the 16th century believed that they were part of a 'Great Chain', created by God.

This Chain stretched from God down to lifeless objects. Everyone and everything had a place in the Chain, with people standing higher than animals, plants and stones. But clergymen and nobles stood higher than gentlemen and peasants, and above them all stood the monarchs.

▲ This German picture from 1532 shows the Chain in the form of a tree. Notice the peasants at the top as well as at the bottom!

▼ All over England, ordinary folk were kept under control by men like these.

Taille (tax on people)

Seigneurial dues

Gabelle (tax on salt)

Tithe

◀ Even if a French peasant farmer was working a fertile plot of land and grew good harvests, the crops and any money he gained from their sale were not all his own. He had to pay many taxes, dues to his local lord, and one-tenth of his income went to the Church.

If you accepted your place on Earth, you were doing God's will, and would be rewarded in Heaven. But if you rebelled against your 'superiors', you were also disobeying God, and could expect dreadful punishments after death.

Therefore, most of those who found themselves near the bottom of the Chain chose to put up with misery on Earth, rather than risk the torments of Hell.

▼ In 1525 a penny (1d) bought 10 eggs, 3.5 litres of milk, 6 herrings, a chicken, and 4 small loaves of bread.

▼ In 1525 a groat (4d) bought half a kilo of beef, a kilo of mutton, a pair of shoes, a kilo of candles, 1.5 litres of wine, and a kilo of soap.

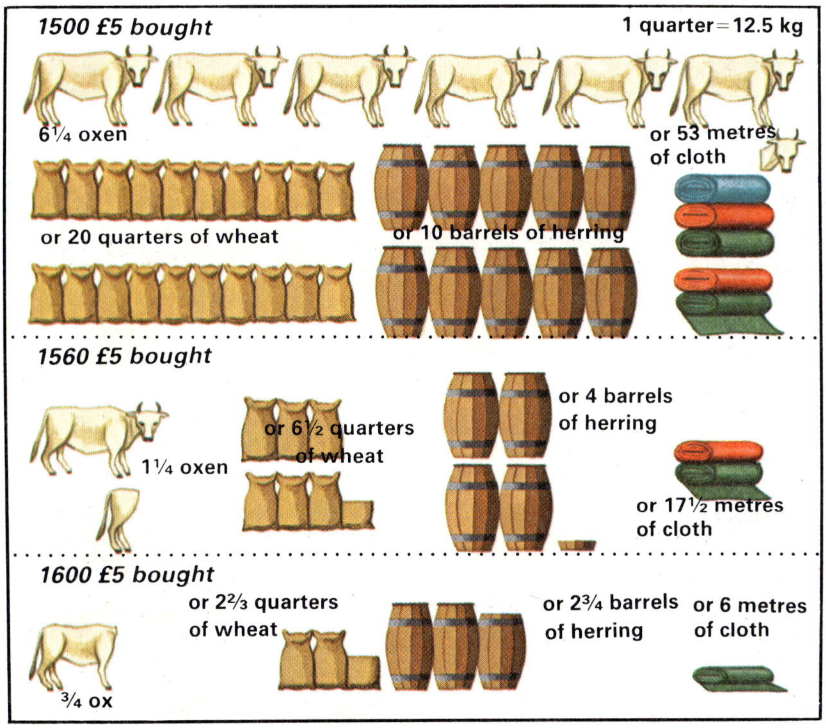

◀ Prices rose very fast in the 16th century. The chart shows the difference between what £5 (a very large sum in those days) bought in 1500, in 1560, and in 1600.

Health and hygiene

No matter where people stood in the 'Great Chain', they lived in the midst of disease and death. Influenza, smallpox and bubonic plague swept across Europe. The worst effects were felt in towns and cities, where large numbers of people were crowded together in filthy conditions. In 1599 alone, plague killed all but 500 of the 4500 inhabitants of Santander in Spain.

Doctors could not explain these diseases, let alone cure them. When Milan was hit by plague in 1576, the blame was placed on 'servants of the devil', who were supposed to have dropped poison into the holy water in the churches.

Doctors and surgeons could deal only with less mysterious ailments. Those who could not afford to pay doctors' fees used herbs as cures. They probably recovered more quickly than some doctors' patients, who were told to swallow crabs' eyes, buttered live spiders or powdered human skull!

By modern standards, 16th century people were hopelessly unhygienic. Soap was very expensive, and people rarely washed. 'The more the dirt is moved,' one Englishman believed, 'the more it stinketh.' Even kings like Henry IV of France had to use special perfumes to drown their dreadful body odours. We can imagine what their subjects smelled like!

▲ Wash-day for some German peasant women. The cloth is being boiled, beaten and rinsed, then hung out to dry, or laid out in the sun to bleach.

▼ Barber-shops were sometimes surgeries too. Here, one barber-surgeon has pulled out a bad tooth, while another is sawing off part of a poisoned leg. Patients had to go through operations without painkillers. The customer on the right is having the lice removed from his scalp.

Surgical instruments

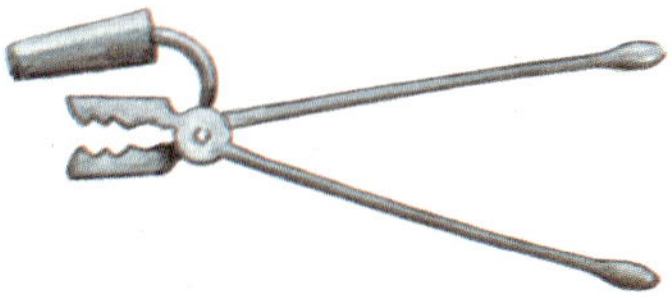

▲ An extractor, used for pulling out teeth.

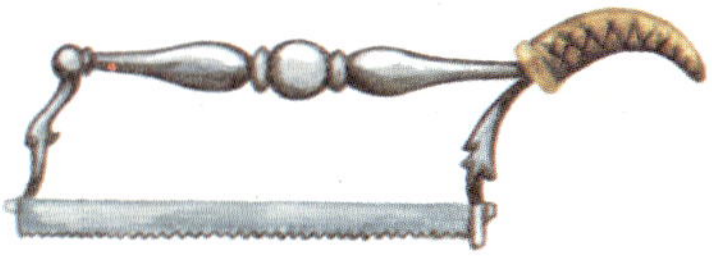

▲ A saw, used for cutting off diseased limbs.

▲ Forceps, used during operations.

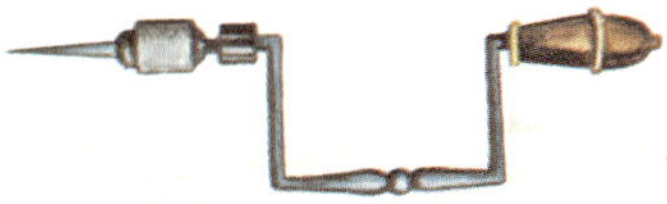

▲ A surgical drill, operated by hand.

▲ The Netherlander Pieter Bruegel painted this extraordinary picture in 1562. It is called *The Triumph of Death*, and is meant to show how violent and dangerous life could be. The skeletons are the army of the dead, who have come back to Earth to carry off the living. Diseases, disasters, famines and wars caused people to die early all over Europe.

◀ Many barber-surgeons had few proper qualifications for their work. They just relied on 'a good eye and a steadfast hand'. Their medical instruments look rather primitive. It was hard to keep them clean in a dirty surgery.

Costume

Costume in the 16th century was not just a matter of personal taste. Queen Elizabeth I of England collected wardrobes full of magnificent dresses, many of them encrusted with precious stones. She dazzled her subjects into obedience with outfits like her white silk dress 'bordered with pearls the size of beans'. Most of those subjects had to make do with simple woollen clothes, which they often made themselves.

Few people could afford to dress fashionably. For most of the century, wealthy men and women copied the styles worn at the Spanish court. Then, towards the end of the century, they began to look to France for new ideas. There were no fashion magazines, but by 1600, small dolls dressed in the latest French styles were being sent from Paris to those who wanted to keep in touch with the trends.

Ruff

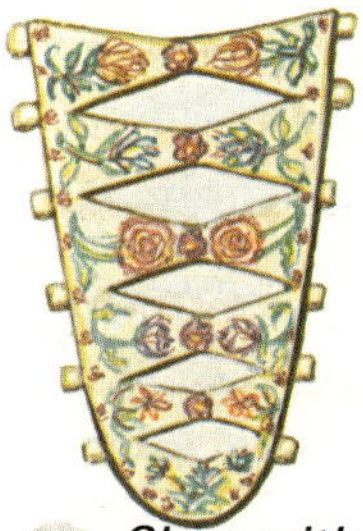

Stomacher

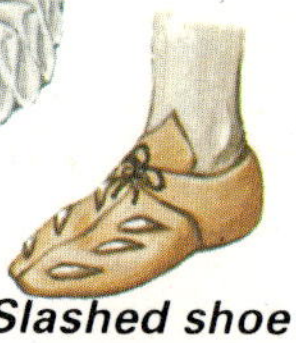

Slashed shoe

Shoe with cork heel

Farthingale

Breeches

◄ Queen Elizabeth I. Like all fashionable ladies, Elizabeth made great use of cosmetics. Bright red lips on a snow-white face were thought to be very beautiful.

French gentleman

◀ **Fashionable clothes were expensive and impractical. Elegant, but flimsy, shoes were made of velvet, silk or soft leather. Women's stomachers and men's breeches were covered with lavish embroidery. Sometimes they were slashed, to show off different material underneath. Women wore frames called 'farthingales' under their gowns, to make the skirts stand out.**

People's clothes showed where they stood in the 'Great Chain'. The rulers of Europe tried to keep their subjects in their proper places by passing laws saying who could wear what. In Paris during the reign of Henry IV, for example, only noblewomen could wear silk. But it was difficult to make people obey such laws. 'There is now such a mingle-mangle of apparel [dress],' an Englishman complained in 1585, 'that it is very hard to know who is noble, who is worshipful, who is a gentleman and who is not.'

▲ **German peasants outside an inn. They are wearing simple, practical outfits in cheap materials. Hats were very popular.**

▼ **Richer people like these dressed to catch the eye. Poorer people could not afford silks, satins, velvets and furs.**

Italian couple

Dutch merchant's wife

English lady with her children

Houses and homes

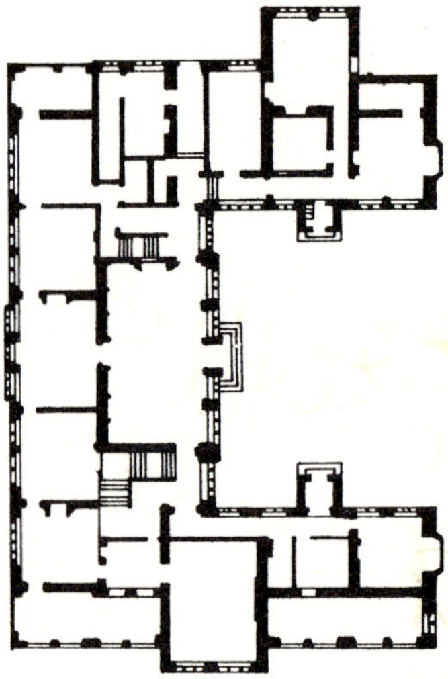

▲ This is a bird's-eye view of Aston Hall, in Warwickshire. Great houses were often built in the shape of the letter 'E'.

In the Middle Ages, the houses of the nobles were built for protection. Inside their thick stone walls masters and servants lived together. But at the end of the 15th century, things started to change. The new cannons could break down even the thickest walls. So the nobles decided that if their homes could not be safe, they might as well be elegant and comfortable. Starting in Italy, a craze for home-improvement and new building spread across Europe.

Wealthy merchants, country gentlemen and prosperous farmers joined the nobles in their building-spree. They used a variety of materials – timber and plaster, stone, and even brick. Glass had become cheaper and more plentiful than before. Windows grew to such a size and number that a house like Hardwick Hall, in England, was said to have 'more glass than wall.' Many houses were also fitted with ornamental chimneys, to take away smoke from the fireplace.

The French and Italians were the first to divide their big

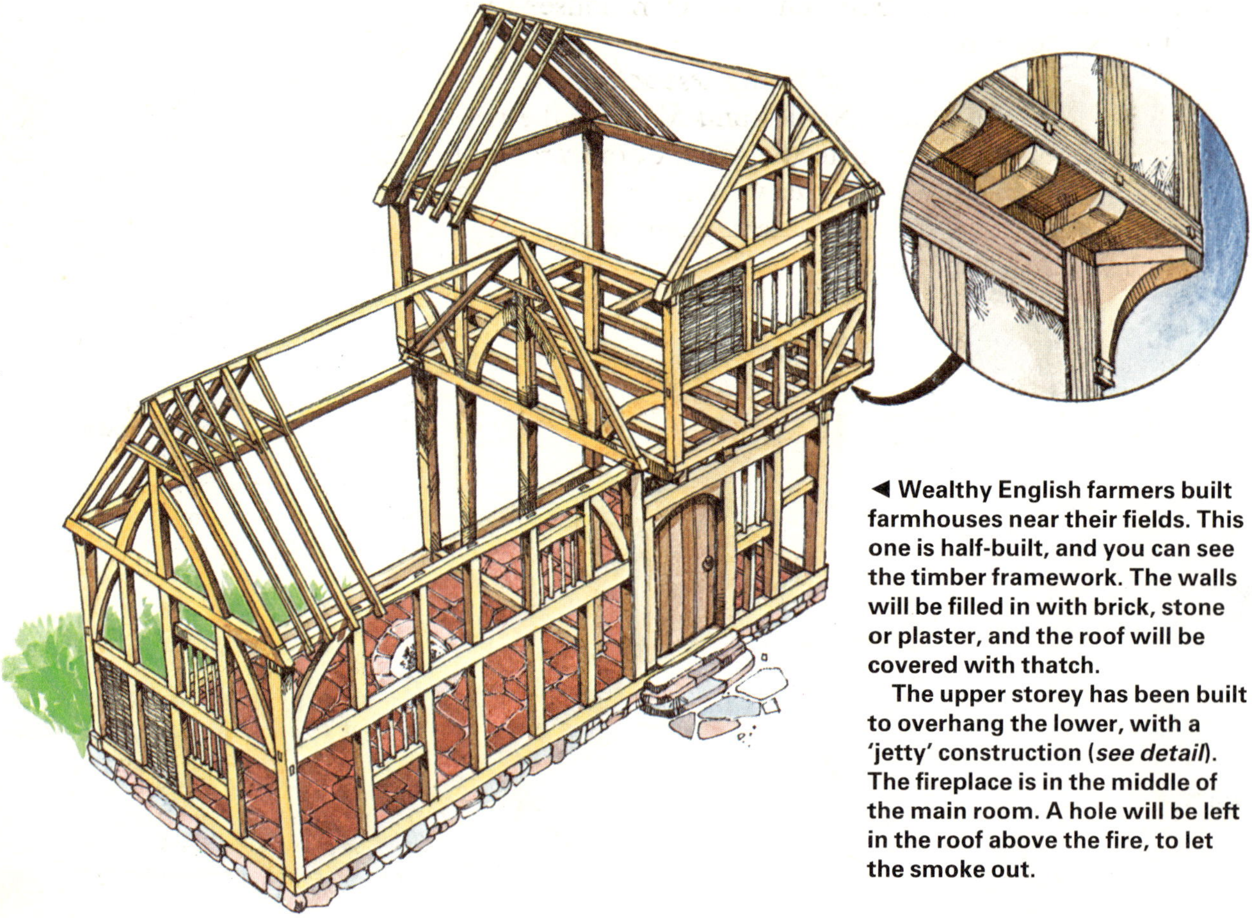

◀ Wealthy English farmers built farmhouses near their fields. This one is half-built, and you can see the timber framework. The walls will be filled in with brick, stone or plaster, and the roof will be covered with thatch.

The upper storey has been built to overhang the lower, with a 'jetty' construction (*see detail*). The fireplace is in the middle of the main room. A hole will be left in the roof above the fire, to let the smoke out.

◀ These peasants have a bare but quite comfortable home, with a separate room for their animals. Many French peasants still lived in one room with their livestock.

The windows are covered with linen, soaked in oil to make it transparent. Glass was still too expensive for most people.

houses into smaller rooms. Ceilings were put in, to make two floors where there had been only one. Upstairs, bedrooms were made. Parlours and kitchens were separated off from other rooms. The French habit of putting the servants' quarters in the basements of town houses soon caught on in London.

But very few people benefited from these improvements. In large cities like London, Naples and Madrid, the new houses of the rich stood next to the squalid, overcrowded dwellings of the poor. While the wealthy were building separate rooms for their servants, many peasants still had to sleep and eat alongside their pigs and cattle.

▲ Some 16th-century merchants' houses are still standing in Amsterdam, Holland. They are closely packed together, and are very close to water. This was convenient, since journeys by water were usually much quicker and safer than journeys by land.

◀ This is the beautiful château at Chenonceaux, in the valley of the Loire river in France. A château is a great country mansion, or even a small castle. This one was begun in 1515. In the past, water had been used for defensive moats. In the 16th century, it was used more often for decoration.

Furniture and furnishings

The poor could afford only the bare necessities of life. Furniture was a luxury. When someone died, an 'inventory' or list of his possessions was made. Inventories which have survived show us how little furniture was owned by the poor – perhaps only a table, a bench, and a few sacks of straw to sleep on. Decoration inside the home was out of the question.

But further up the 'Great Chain', the insides of people's houses were changing. The large glass windows let more light into the rooms, so people with money wanted to buy furniture that was beautiful to look at as well as useful.

The parlour was usually the most finely-decorated room. It might have carved wooden panelling on the walls, plaster patterns on the ceiling, and even colourful coats-of-arms in the windows. Carpets and tapestries were draped over solid, wooden tables and chests. On the floor, rushes were scattered in winter, and herbs and flowers in the summer.

▲ Bedwarmers like these could be put under the bedclothes. The top one is a pan, which was filled with hot coals. The other one is a candle in a wooden cage.

▼ This four-poster bed is made of solid oak, and probably has a feather mattress. Two curtains pull right round the bed, to keep out draughts. The master's oak chair has arms, which were gradually coming into fashion.

► Most rulers liked to surround themselves with beautiful furnishings and ornaments. The Italian Benvenuto Cellini made this salt-cellar and gave it to Francis I of France in 1543. 'The King cried aloud in astonishment and could not look at it long enough', wrote Cellini afterwards.

▼ People used cut-away beer-barrels for tables and chairs. They were especially common in Dutch inns.

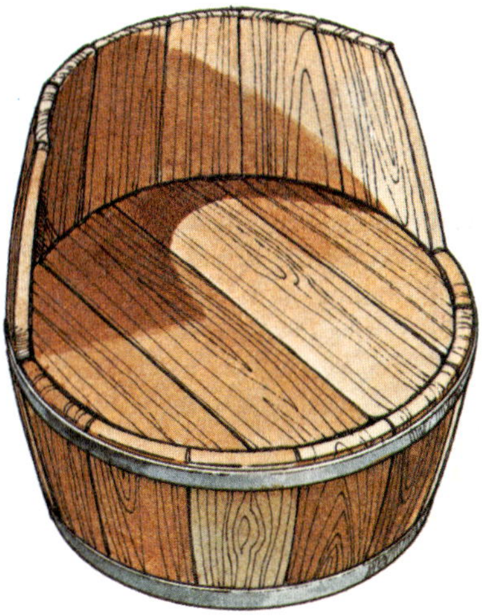

If these were not changed regularly, they could collect dirt, and smell badly. The Dutch scholar, Erasmus, complained about the dreadful state of English floors.

By today's standards, houses were not very comfortable. Chairs with arms or padding were rare. There were no indoor toilets or bathrooms. Even the most luxurious houses were both cold and smelly.

But the well-to-do cared more about appearances than comfort, in their houses as well as in their clothes.

► Tudor furniture was built to last. These handcarved pieces are all made of oak. At first, they were light in colour. Years of wear, and beeswax polishing, have turned them dark brown.

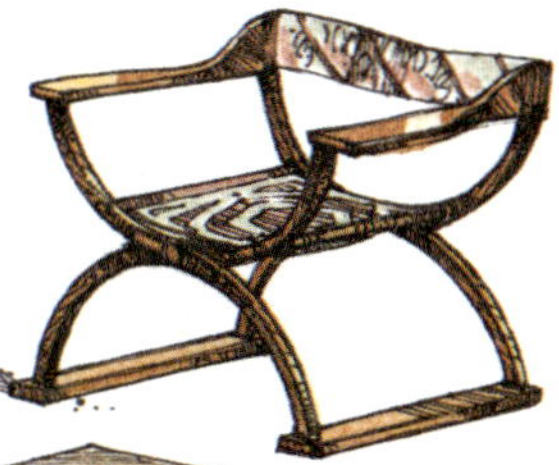

Food and drink

Most peasant diets were unbalanced and boring. In an age of rocketing prices, the poor could afford little more than bread, made from wheat, barley or rye. Sometimes the bread was stirred into watery vegetable stews. But meat was too expensive for most people. Fruit was quite common in southern Europe, even though doctors believed it caused fevers. Since people depended on bread, one bad harvest could cause widespread starvation. There were thirteen major famines in this century in France alone. At such times, the hungry would eat almost anything – straw, roots, rats, even tree-bark!

By contrast, the rich ate an enormous variety of meats and fish. Meat was often dried and salted, to keep it through the winter. Then it was cooked in hot spices – to cover up the taste and smell of decay. Most vegetables were despised by the rich, although cabbages were thought to prevent baldness.

New delicacies like turkeys and drinking chocolate, both from Mexico, provided variety now and then. Sugar was still a luxury. It was expensive, and difficult to obtain. When available, it was sprinkled on everything, including meat.

▲ **Carriers like this man sold water to many homes. The water was used more often for cooking than for washing.**

▼ **Special rooms were now set aside for eating. People ate with their hands, from pewter plates. Poorer families used wooden plates.**

Suggestions for elaborate dishes could be found in cookery books, such as *The Boke of Kerving*, published in England in 1508. But France was already becoming recognised as the home of fine cooking.

The people of southern Europe drank enormous amounts of wine. In about the middle of the 16th century, each citizen of Valladolid in Spain consumed around a hundred litres a year. In northern Europe, home-brewed beer and sometimes cider were commonly drunk by both adults and children.

▲ Spanish nobles, or 'grandees', ate extremely well. They had delicacies imported from both Europe and America.

Their guests brought their own knives. They needed them, to cope with the many meat dishes. In the year 1600 alone, 50,000 sheep, 12,000 oxen, 60,000 kids, 10,000 calves and 13,000 pigs were eaten in Madrid.

Family life

Half of all the children born in the 16th century died before reaching their first birthdays. Those who survived were often killed at an early age by famine, disease or war. Therefore the people of Europe were astonished to see that the population was growing very fast. Many were worried that Europe was getting overcrowded. However, there were far fewer people than there are today. There are perhaps ten times as many people in the British Isles now as there were in 1600!

Anyone over 40 years of age was thought to be old. Children made up about half the population in most countries. 'The whole of Germany is teeming with children,' wrote Sebastian Franck in 1538. All these young people had to be kept in order. The father of the household was expected to rule his family as a king ruled his subjects. This meant that he often arranged marriages for all his children.

Poor people usually got married later than rich people. They also had fewer children. A Flemish proverb said 'Little wealth and many children bring great distress to many a man.'

▲ This old man has made a contract with his children. He has agreed to give them his property, as long as they care for him until he dies. Some families did not look after their older members, unless a contract like this had been made.

◄ Babies were christened very soon after they were born. This was because so many babies died, and their parents wanted to feel sure that their souls would go straight to heaven. There were no birth certificates in the 16th century, so many grown-up people were not sure exactly how old they were.

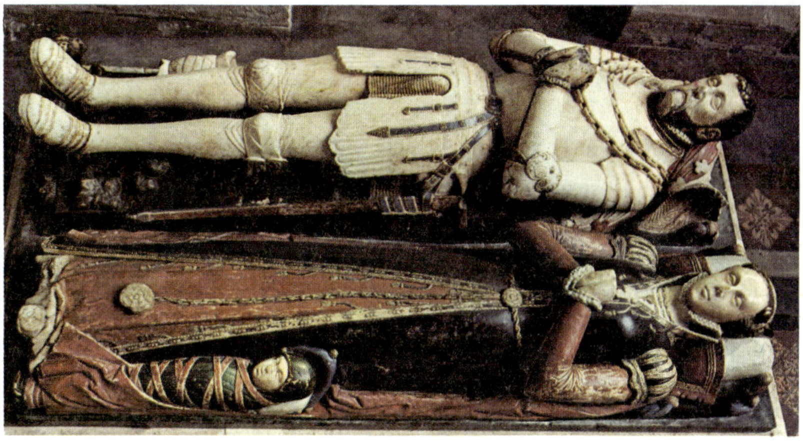

► This beautifully-coloured tomb is in Hereford Cathedral. The figures on top are models of the three people who are buried inside. The man is Alexander Denton, a gentleman who died in 1576 at the age of 31. The woman is his second wife, Anne, who died in 1566, when she was only 17. She died while giving birth to their child, who is also buried in the tomb. Only a wealthy family could have afforded an expensive tomb like this.

Men controlled their wives almost as closely as their children. A bookseller from Florence, in Italy, thought that all women should obey two rules: 'the first is that they should bring up their children in the fear of God, and the second that they keep quiet in Church.' Compared to southern Europe, England was called 'a paradise for married women.' But even here, the Church taught that woman 'was made for the man's use and benefit' – which usually meant a lifetime of domestic chores and child-bearing.

▼ Once they were married, women were often expected to have a baby each year. They also had to run their households. Better-off women might have a nurse to look after their babies, and servants to help in the house, but there was still a great deal to do. These are just some of a woman's household jobs.

Preserving fish and meat for the winter

Baking bread

Shopping

Cooking and mending

Carding (right) and spinning wool

Going to school

An Elizabethan schoolmaster called Richard Mulcaster wrote that the point of education was to train every person 'to perform those functions in life which his position shall require'. Most people needed no book-learning to carry out their daily duties, so they received little or no education. Women were expected to content themselves with household work, so girls too were rarely educated.

There were many schools for the sons of the nobility and the middle classes. At the start of the century, most schools were attached to churches or monasteries. In these 'grammar-schools', boys whose parents wanted them to go to university, or to become priests, learned almost nothing but Latin grammar. There were few books, so long passages had to be learned by heart. Lessons could go on for ten hours a day, six days a week. The boys had to speak Latin, as well as to write it, and could be punished for speaking their own language. Even small offences were severely punished. A pupil might receive more than fifty strokes of the birch in a single day.

▼ Schoolmasters had no special training for their work. They were often priests. Tudor schoolboys like these had to sit through 1,826 hours of lessons a year. No wonder holidays were sometimes called 'remedies'!

◄ This is Saint Ignatius Loyola (1491–1556). He set up many Jesuit schools in the Catholic parts of Europe. He was so interested in teaching and children, that he was made the patron saint of women who were expecting babies.

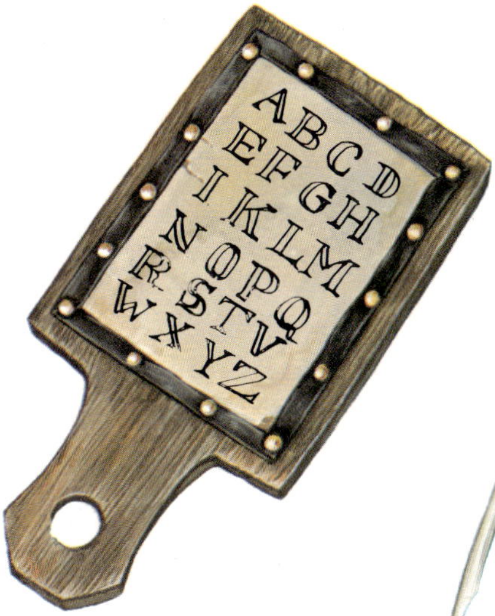

► Children often began their education with a 'horn-book' like this. Inside the wooden frame was a single page, which was protected by a thin, clear sheet of horn.

▲ A bird's-feather quill pen for writing. Children usually sharpened their own quills with knives. They were also expected to mix their own ink.

Later in the century noblemen and merchants set up new schools in towns all over Europe. Many teachers stopped beating information into their pupils. Instead they encouraged them to seek knowledge for themselves. Gradually acting, speechmaking, and even dancing and sport started to appear on the timetable. But Latin was still believed to be the most important subject of all.

▼ The Royal Grammar School in Guildford, Surrey, is still standing today, but it was built in Tudor times. Many other English schools are named after King Edward VI, the son of Henry VIII.

Centres of learning

In 16th century England, there were only two universities – Oxford and Cambridge. 'They were erected by their founders,' wrote an Elizabethan, 'only for poor men's sons, whose parents were not able to bring them up unto learning.' In earlier times, these boys had usually gone on to be priests. But all over Europe, the sons of the wealthy were gradually squeezing poorer students out of the centres of learning.

A year or two at college had become a useful stepping-stone towards a career as a lawyer or a doctor, a business-man or a politician. Few of these richer undergraduates studied for long enough to gain a degree. Most of them went to university when they were about fourteen years old, and often got into 'riotous company which draweth them from their books.'

Students were watched over by tutors. A tutor not only taught his students; he also looked after them when they fell sick, handed out their pocket money, and birched them if they misbehaved. In return for all his services, he received payments from their fathers. Poor men simply could not afford to send their sons to university.

Serious students completed the full degree course after seven years. They studied subjects ranging from astronomy and the theory of music to theology. Lectures could begin as early as 6.30 in the morning, and last for as long as two hours. Students were tested in written examinations and also in 'disputations'. These were debates on a set topic between a student and his masters – in Latin.

BIBLIA
The Bible that
is, the holy Scripture of the
Olde and New Testament, faith-
fully and truly translated out
of Douche and Latyn
in to Englishe.
M. D. XXXV.
S. paul. II. Tessa. III.
Praie for vs, that the worde of God maie
have fre passage, and be glorified. &c.
S. paul Col. III.
Let the worde of Christ dwell in you plen
teously in all wysdome &c.
Josue I.
Let not the boke of this lawe departe
out of thy mouth, but exercyse thyselfe
therin daye and nighte &c.

▲ Catholics used Latin Bibles. But the Protestants believed that the Bible should be put into everyday language, so that more people would be able to understand it. A scholar called Miles Coverdale was the first man to put the whole Bible into English, and to have it printed. This is the title-page of his English Bible of 1535.

◄ The University of Salamanca, in Spain, was one of the greatest in 16th-century Europe. It had started as a cathedral school in the 13th century.

► Henry VIII's chief minister, Cardinal Thomas Wolsey, paid for this Oxford college to be built. He called it Cardinal College, after himself, but Henry later re-named it King's College. Eventually it was given its present name, Christ Church. The loud bell in this tower is still called 'Great Tom', after the Cardinal.

◄ This Oxford student is nearing the end of his seven-year course, when he will qualify as a Master of Arts. Many students had to pay for their own board and lodging. Poorer students raised money by doing odd jobs around the College, or by begging.

Work in the fields

In 1600, only about one European in every ten lived in a town. But the country-workers had to provide food and clothing for the townspeople, as well as for themselves. 'Whosoever doth not maintain the plough destroys this kingdom,' remarked Lord Burghley, Elizabeth I's chief minister.

The country-worker's day often began at dawn, and ended when it grew too dark to see. At sowing, ploughing and harvesting times, work could go on far into the night. Bread crops (wheat, barley, rye and oats), meat and milk were produced all over Europe. Other types of food varied from region to region. Cheese, bacon and lard were common in the north. Oil, wine, fruit and beans were often produced in the south. Wool and hides, which could be made into clothing, came from livestock everywhere.

Some new crops were beginning to appear in Europe. Maize was imported from America, and grown in northern

► The owner of these fields separated his grazing land from his crop land. He 'enclosed' the fields with hedges. Sheep-farming had become very profitable, and farmers needed more pasture for their extra flocks. Sometimes they enclosed 'common land', which had once been used by poor peasants for their animals as well.

▼ The women on the left are picking vegetables called artichokes. They were believed to make people feel romantic!

The masked beekeeper (*centre*) had no trouble selling his honey. It was used to sweeten food, before sugar became available.

The men on the right are harvesting hops, which are used to make beer.

◀ This woodcut shows activities on a farm in spring. In the background the soil is being harrowed to break it up, and in front a man is sowing seed by scattering it as he walks along the furrows.

Italy. The potato had also been introduced from the New World. But farming remained very old-fashioned throughout Europe. Wooden farm-tools had hardly changed in hundreds of years. Few people owned a plough, and fewer still owned a team of cattle to pull the plough, and to supply manure to enrich the soil. Bread crops could not be grown on the same land for two years running. The soil had to be left untouched, to allow it to get back its richness. Therefore large fields lay unused for a year or more.

There was no shortage of new books on how to farm more efficiently. But very few men could read them. So farming remained backward, and famines were inevitable now and then.

▲ Ploughs were made of wood, and were often operated by hand. In the middle picture opposite, you can see two men furrowing the soil with one. But many poor peasant farmers could not afford even such simple tools.

▼ In autumn everyone helped to get the hay in before rain could spoil it. Hay was very important as feed for livestock during the winter. Most European people were involved in farmwork of some sort.

Vagabonds and bandits

Vagabonds were people who either could not or would not find work for themselves. They took to the roads and begged or thieved. Many of them drifted into the larger towns, which were already overcrowded. Others ended up fighting for pay in armies all over Europe.

The population was rising so fast that there was a lot of competition for jobs. Most vagabonds just wandered around the country until they found work. But some people actually chose to beg and steal. They made governments believe that *all* vagabonds were 'loathsomely idle'. Anyone caught begging was therefore punished harshly. In England, a vagabond could be branded on the cheek with a 'V', and sent back to his home parish. But the Poor Law of 1601 made arrangements for the old and the sick to be cared for, and for work to be found for the able-bodied.

In southern Europe, the problem was more serious. When times were bad, hungry peasants flocked to join bandit gangs in the mountains and forests. They lived by robbing people. Governments tried to control them by using violence themselves. 'This year,' said a Roman newsletter of 1585, 'we have seen more heads on show on the Sant Angelo bridge than melons in the market.'

▼ Some beggars were wounded ex-soldiers. Others just pretended to be crippled, to win sympathy. Large towns attracted both beggars and those who really wanted to work. Therefore, the local authorities in large English towns made the earliest attempts to provide help for the poor.

► Travelling pedlars tramped the roads of Europe, selling cheap goods. This painting is by the Netherlander Hieronymus Bosch, who died early in the 16th century. The pedlar, in his odd shoes, looks terribly shabby. The house in the background needs repairing. Paintings like this remind us how poor many people were.

▼ The roads of Europe were plagued by bandit gangs. These highwaymen were sometimes in league with innkeepers, who provided rooms for travellers. There were no police forces to fight crime like this. But any bandits who were caught could expect little mercy.

Crime and punishment

Punishments in the 16th century seem terribly harsh to us. In England, you could be slowly strangled to death for stealing goods worth more than one shilling. In parts of Italy, you could have your tongue ripped out for using the Lord's name as a swear-word. But many criminals were never caught. There were no detectives or policemen to track them down. So when a criminal *was* caught, he was severely punished, to make it clear to others that crime did not pay. This is why executions were held in public.

Violence was more widespread than it is today. In the larger towns and cities, most people went about armed, to defend themselves against sudden attacks or robberies. Torture was the usual way of getting information out of criminals. It seemed quite natural that murderers or traitors should be hung, burned or boiled to death.

But criminals who had committed offences like stealing were often spared the harsh punishments laid down by law. In England, juries sometimes allowed thieves to go free instead of demanding the death penalty. 'The simple countrymen and women are of opinion that they would not bring about a man's death for all the goods in the world,' said a royal servant in 1596.

▲ Many small offences were punished by death. But for crimes like cheating customers at the market, wrongdoers could be put in the local stocks (*above*) or pillory (*below*).

▲ The stains on the pillory were made by rotten vegetables and eggs, hurled by passers-by. Some wrongdoers had their ears nailed to the wood.

◄ This man is being punished for begging without a licence. According to a Tudor Act of Parliament, such men had to be 'tied to the end of a cart naked and beaten with whips throughout the town till their bodies be bloody'.

► At the front of this German picture, a criminal is being condemned to death. In the background, you can see some of the horrific ways in which he could be punished. These include being burned alive and being left to rot on a wheel. Look at the picture on page 17 to see men tied to wheels on the tops of poles.

Even if a man was not let off by the jury, he could ask for 'benefit of clergy'. In the 16th century, this meant that if a man could pass a reading test, he was just branded and handed over to the local bishop. Then he usually received a mild punishment, and was released.

▼ Mary Queen of Scots calmly awaits her execution at Fotheringay Castle, Northamptonshire, England, in 1587. She was condemned to death for plotting to seize the English Crown from her cousin, Queen Elizabeth I. Death by beheading was quick, as long as the axe struck firmly and strongly first time. Criminals from lower down the Chain suffered the slower death of hanging.

Witchcraft

The 16th century was a time of great hardship and suffering. Many people believed that 'servants of the devil' caused illness, death and famine. 'Witches' were thought to be the devil's helpers. It was easy to blame witches for disasters. More people were hunted down and burned as witches in the 16th century than at any time before. This did not stop disasters happening however.

There was no *proof* that witches put curses on cattle, or killed people by magic spells. But governments and ordinary people blamed them all the same. The main problem was how to identify the witches. They could be men or children, but usually they were thought to be women. This was because women were generally thought to be the more wicked sex. A woman who seemed different in any way was suspected at once. She might be a young and beautiful girl, or old and ugly. She might be physically deformed, or even mentally ill.

▼ The girl in the chair is being 'ducked' in a river. If she does not drown, she must be a witch, because the devil is helping her to float. The male 'witch' below is being filled up with water. Eventually he will admit that he is a witch, just to stop the torture. The deformed girl who is being stretched will do the same. In England convicted witches were punished by hanging. They were suspended by their necks until they slowly strangled to death.

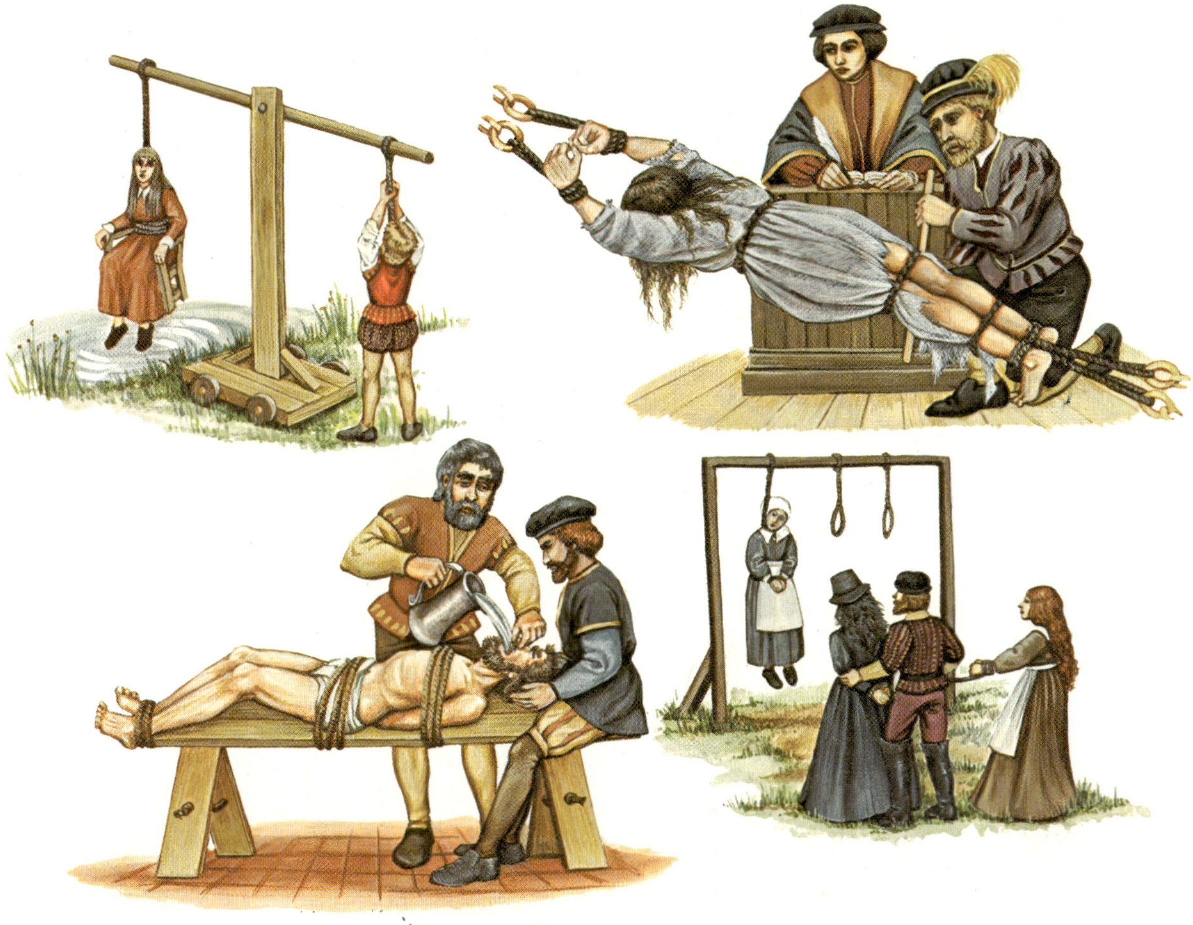

► In 1607 Frans Francken the Younger painted this picture of a witches' 'Sabbath', or midnight meeting. It shows many of the things witches were supposed to do, such as casting spells, flying on broomsticks, and signing agreements with the devil. People believed that meetings like this really took place!

Suspects were tortured until they admitted to crimes that they had never committed. The instruments of torture were horrific. The leg screw, used a lot in Scotland and Germany, slowly squeezed the calf until the shin-bone was shattered to pieces. Under such torture, women 'confessed' to all sorts of crimes. Then they were executed.

Hundreds of thousands of innocent women were killed during the great 'witch-craze'. The frenzy gripped even intellectuals like the French philosopher Jean Bodin. He demanded that anyone who refused to *believe* in witches should be burned at the stake! This might seem incredible to us. But when times are hard, people often pick on those who are least able to defend themselves.

▼ In France, young girls and old women alike were burned as witches. Henri Boguet, a French lawyer, roared 'All over Europe, this miserable and damnable vermin is multiplying on the land like caterpillars in a garden. I wish they had but one body, so that we could burn them all at once, in one fire!'

Popular entertainment

During the working week, there was little time for leisure. But Sundays, Saints' Days, and the great festivals of Christmas, Easter and Whitsuntide allowed people to relax and enjoy themselves.

They danced, drank, sang, and played games like draughts, dice, cards and chess. For those who wanted more bloodthirsty pleasures, there were bear-baiting, cock-fighting and, in the streets of southern Europe, bull-fighting. Whole villages played a violent form of football, which was less of a game than 'a friendly kind of fight'. The most revolting entertainment of all was the public torture and execution of criminals.

▼ In this Elizabethan theatre, the players are performing Shakespeare's *A Midsummer Night's Dream*. Performances had to take place in daylight, because it was hard to light the theatre after dark. The flag was raised to announce a play that afternoon. The trumpeters in the little tower heralded the start with a fanfare. There was very little scenery on the stage, and boys played the parts of women.

◀ Some common pastimes in Tudor England: (1) cock-fighting, (2) football, (3) bear-baiting, (4) dancing around the maypole and (5) playing cards in the tavern. All these remained popular for at least two more centuries.

▼ This is a close-up of part of a painting from 1560. It is called *Children's Games*, and was painted by Pieter Bruegel. Some of the games shown are still played today. Notice how some of the players look much more like miniature grown-ups than children.

Most people could not read, but enjoyed listening to preachers and actors. Thousands of people gathered to watch religious 'mystery plays'. Less holy plays were put on by bands of travelling-players, in market squares and inn yards. But these actors were often treated by the local authorities as little better than vagabonds. Towards the end of the century proper theatres were built in the larger towns and cities of Europe. In these places, packed audiences were thrilled by the plays of men like Shakespeare in England, and Lope da Vega in Spain. Today we might think of such playwrights as brilliant intellectuals. But the uneducated people of the 16th century just saw them as first-rate entertainers.

Entertainments for the nobles

We have already seen that the wealthy dressed up, built homes and feasted magnificently. They also enjoyed many of the same entertainments as the poor, like dancing and theatre-going.

But nobles had more leisure-time than those lower down the Chain. In the Middle Ages, their main purpose in life had been to fight in their rulers' armies. But now most wars were being fought by humbler, paid soldiers. New laws forbade the nobles to feud among themselves, so they had to find other ways of getting rid of their energies. They turned to massive hunting expeditions – and to duelling. Duels were fought for the slightest reasons. Between 1585 and 1603, the Kings of France pardoned no less than 7,000 duellists who had killed their opponents.

► The virginal, or spinet, was a favourite instrument of Queen Elizabeth I.

▲ The viol was held upright between the knees and played with a bow.

▲ Lutes were sometimes provided in barbershops for waiting gentlemen to play.

▼ Gentlemen practising their marksmanship. They are shooting crossbow-bolts at small birds tied to the top of a pole. The man at the front is holding a longbow.

But the nobles of Europe spent only part of their time killing animals or one another. They enjoyed games, like indoor tennis, and they gambled passionately. Many nobles were also patrons of the arts. This meant that they paid musicians, artists and craftsmen to come to their homes and produce works of art for them.

The greatest providers of entertainment were the rulers of Europe. The nobles flocked regularly to their rulers' courts, to take part in lavish ceremonial pageants, masques, jousts and mock-battles. The rulers had good reason to attract their most important subjects to court. While the nobles were busy enjoying themselves, they had no time to feud against one another, or to plot against their rulers.

▼ Woodwind instruments. *Top*: a shawm, rather like an oboe. *Below*: a wooden recorder.

▼ Trumpets did not have valves. They were called natural trumpets.

► Musicians were employed to play at lavish balls and masques.

► Outdoors, hunting was very popular. These men are hunting otters. Gentlemen – and gentlewomen – chased deer, hares, bustards, foxes and badgers as well.

▼ Rulers and their nobles enjoyed jousting tournaments. But some bouts ended in tragedy. In 1559, King Henry II of France received a lance-wound in the eye. He was dead within a few days.

A soldier's life

The mightiest armies of the 16th century served King Philip II of Spain. Most of his soldiers were poor men from all over Europe, who hoped to win great fortunes by capturing rich prisoners, or by ransacking a town of its treasures after a siege. While they were in the army they did not pay taxes, tithes or rents. They were given food, shelter, clothing, and hospital treatment. Such a life appealed to men further up the Chain too. One of the footsoldiers in the Spanish army in the Netherlands in 1595 was the English gentleman, Guy Fawkes.

But a soldier's life was usually boring and miserable. His officers despised him, and could fine, flog or humiliate him as they chose. Wages were almost always late, food and clothing in short supply, and diseases caused more deaths than enemy attacks. Most of the time was spent in starving one large town after another into surrender. There were few actual battles.

◄ Spanish troops besieging the fortress of St Quentin in the Netherlands, 1557. The siege was followed by a face-to-face battle, won by the Spaniards.

▼ The soldiers of Philip II's forces in the Netherlands in 1588. There were also thousands of women, children, cooks, priests and surgeons.

	Spanish Army 63,455 Soldiers
Infantry	30,211 Netherlanders 11,309 German 9,668 Spaniards 5,339 Italians 1,722 British 1,556 Burgundians
	3,650 Cavalry

Musketeer

Landsknecht, using a two-handed sword

Crossbowman

Fighting with estocs

◀ **The landsknecht was a professional German footsoldier.**

Muskets were now replacing longbows. In the Netherlands, some musketeers had to pay for their own powder and shot. This must have made them think twice before firing!

Worst of all there was no such thing as leave. Soldiers had to agree to serve until the end of the war. Only those who were hopelessly injured were allowed to go home early. Even those who managed to survive could find little work when they got back home, and often had to become vagabonds or bandits.

◀ **Soldiers wore no special uniforms. This Spanish officer is wearing a bright red sash, to show which army he is in.**

▶ **Towns in the Netherlands were often heavily fortified. Philip II's armies could only take them by starving the townspeople. Even small towns could hold out for months.**

Land travel

▲ Coaches had no springs, and were cold and uncomfortable.

▲ A peasant woman rides to market. She was lucky to have the use of a horse. Poorer women made do with donkeys.

Most people rarely travelled far from their birthplaces. In England, Cornishmen regarded anyone from the Midlands as a foreigner. But certain types of people did not spend their whole lives rooted to one place. Rulers regularly moved around their lands, so that their subjects could see them. Travelling players, beggars and pedlars earned their livings on the road; so did messengers, and the carriers of goods. But whether you travelled on foot, on horseback or in a wagon, journeys were always slow and dangerous.

Wherever there were rivers or canals, bulky goods were transported by water. On the roads, pack-horses were used more often than wagons. This was because wheeled vehicles often sank into the winter mud on the badly-kept roads – and had to wait until summer to be dragged out. All travellers were prey to vagabonds and bandits, and in wartime to soldiers as well. They also had to pay 'tolls', or fees, every time their routes crossed the territory of a noble landowner.

The nobles themselves had begun to travel in coaches. These had no springs or glass windows, and were highly uncomfortable for long journeys.

▼ French peasants were forced by law to keep local roads in good repair. But they could do little to stop them from turning into quagmires in winter.

► This map shows how quickly post-horses could carry news across Europe. Ordinary travellers made slower progress. But they were helped by many new printed maps and guidebooks.

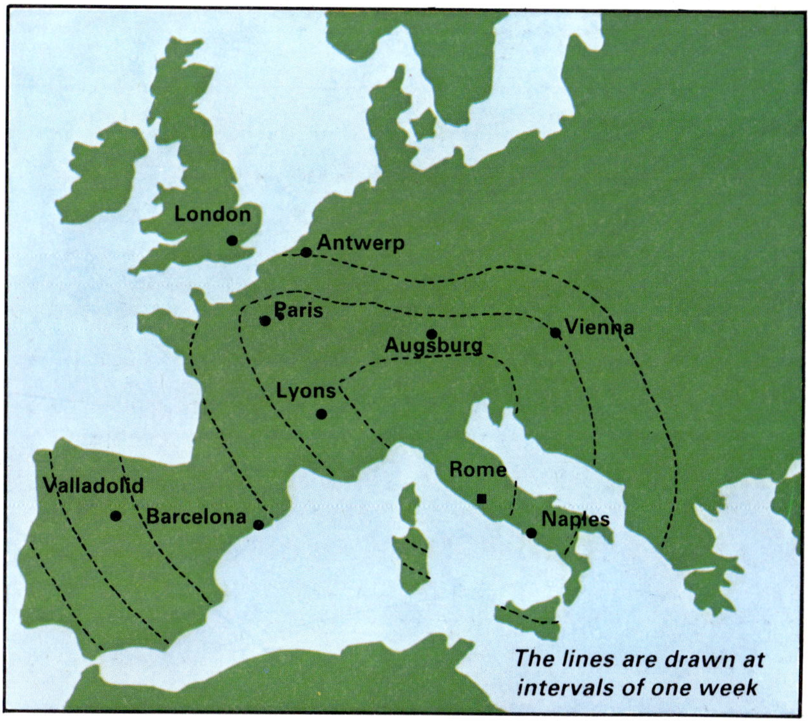

▼ Queen Elizabeth I travelling on the Thames by barge. She never went more than a hundred miles (160 km) from London during her reign.

The small picture shows an earlier barge on the river Rhine in Germany, in 1531.

Although people were travelling as slowly as ever in the 16th century, news was travelling much faster. The map above shows how quickly post-horses could gallop around Europe. Yet the European postal service was far slower than the system which the Spaniards discovered in Peru. There, relays of men could carry messages over distances of 150 miles (240 km) a day – all on foot!

Sailors and the sea

Before the 16th century, almost all seaborne trade was carried on in the Mediterranean, using *galleys*: long, thin vessels driven by oarsmen. Then, in the 16th century, Europeans began to trade with faraway peoples. The Spaniards and the Portuguese built huge sailing ships, called 'galleons', to cross the oceans. Many sailors died on these voyages. Some were killed by pirates or storms, others by disease, often caused by bad food. A survivor of Magellan's voyage around the world recalled, 'We ate biscuit, but in truth it was biscuit no longer but a powder full of worm, and in addition it was stinking with the urine of rats.'

Another danger for these merchant fleets was 'privateers'. These were privately-owned English, French

► Sailors on the cramped gun-deck of a galleon. One is mending a torn sail, made of hide. Another is eating dried biscuit and salted fish. Sailors often suffered badly from fevers and scurvy, caused by the lack of fresh vegetables or fruit. On long voyages, stored water went bad. It had to be strained through a cloth, to filter off the stinking scum.

▼ On early galleons the cannons could only be fired at very close quarters. So battles like this one were still decided by the soldiers on board, fighting hand-to-hand.

or Dutch ships, whose captains had been given royal permission to seize and plunder enemy vessels. The galleons used heavy cannon to fend off the smaller, faster privateers. But English 'sea-dogs', like Sir Francis Drake, still raided Spanish ports and fleets with great success.

In the 1580s, war broke out between England and Spain. Queen Elizabeth I put the privateer captains in charge of the galleons of the Royal Navy. Their crews were taken from merchant ships. Yet this makeshift fleet was able to shatter and scatter the great Spanish Armada of 1588.

▲ Small vessels sailing to America or the East Indies could not always keep land in sight.

Navigators used simple instruments like these to work out where they were.

Merchants and traders

'The purpose of every merchant,' wrote an Italian mathematician, 'is to make a lawful and reasonable profit so as to keep up his business.' In the 16th century, the profits from worldwide trade could be huge. The nobles, especially in southern Europe, despised rich merchants. 'Inherited wealth is more honest than earned wealth,' they believed, 'in view of the vile gain needed to obtain the latter.' But the rulers of Europe were less proud. Kings and Emperors were often glad to borrow money from the greatest merchant families, like the Fuggers of Augsburg.

Many merchants clubbed together in trade companies, like the Merchant Adventurers of London. Sometimes these companies were granted royal 'monopolies'. These were charters allowing only one company to trade in certain goods, or with a certain region. Thus only the Merchant Adventurers could export English cloth to the Netherlands.

▼ Cheaper goods from abroad could reach local markets like this one. But food travelled badly over long distances, unless it was first dried and salted. Most people still ate only locally-produced food.

◀ A rich woman visiting a London tailor. One apprentice is cutting lengths from a roll of silk imported from Italy. The master will then cut the silk into the shape of a dress. The other apprentices are stitching together pieces of a different garment.

The Muscovy Company was given a monopoly of trade with Russia, and the Eastland Company with ports in the Baltic. By 1600, a few companies based in London were handling almost all England's foreign trade.

▼ Pictorial shop-signs like these told people what went on inside shops. They were a great help to those who could not read.

Locksmith

Tailor

► Coins were vital for international trade. These coins were hammered out by hand. But after 1550, more and more European coins were pressed by machines.

Brushmaker

Fishmonger

Groat (English)

Piece-of-eight (Spanish)

Sovereign (English)

Teston (French)

Thaler (Austrian)

Great cities

By 1500, some of Europe's major cities had become very powerful. In Italy cities like Venice and Genoa ruled themselves, and had built up huge trading empires. In the Holy Roman Empire, 'Imperial Free Cities' like Strasburg were virtually outside the Emperor's control. But the monarchs of Spain, France and England kept a much closer check on the great cities in their states.

Throughout the 16th century, European cities attracted more and more people. In 1500, only four of them had more than 100,000 inhabitants – Paris, Naples, Venice and Milan. By 1600, there were at least eight more – Rome, Palermo and Messina in Italy; the national capitals of London and Madrid; and the new trade centres of Lisbon in Portugal, Seville in Spain and Antwerp in the Netherlands.

Rulers began to hold their courts in, or just outside the great cities. Therefore the nobles spent part of each year in their magnificent new town houses, so that they could be close to their powerful rulers. Vagabonds also flooded into the cities, in search of work of any kind. At least half the population of any city lived in real poverty. In times of famine, these people were the first to starve, since they were

▼ This is a 16th-century view of Antwerp, on the river Scheldt in the Netherlands. Antwerp was one of the most important cities in Charles V's empire. It was full of trade depots, banks and industrial workshops. Sadly, in 1576 the Spanish soldiers stationed in Antwerp went berserk. They raided and destroyed a large part of the city, and over 7,000 citizens and soldiers were killed.

unable to grow their own food. Even when there was enough to eat, their drinking water was often poisoned by sewage. This caused epidemics, which raged through the damp, dark, overcrowded slums.

But the cities also had many attractions. There were taverns, and plenty of entertainments. Above all, people dreamed of making their fortunes in the great cities. Unfortunately, very few of them were as successful as Dick Whittington!

▼ **The women at the front of this city-scene are wearing little wooden platforms under their shoes. These are to keep their feet clean and dry. Shopkeepers' wives pour their slops out of windows. An evil-smelling open sewer runs down the middle of the street. The houses are made mainly of wood, and are closely packed together.**

Crafts and industries

The number of skilled craftsmen and industrial labourers was growing steadily at this time. These people provided buildings, clothes and furniture for both rich and poor. They also manufactured the goods which European merchants traded overseas for gold, silver and spices.

In the towns and cities, a craftsman usually belonged to a 'guild'. These organizations had grown up during the Middle Ages. They laid down rules on standards of workmanship, fixed wages and decided on prices for finished goods. They also made sure that apprentices were given proper training by their masters, and looked after members who had fallen on hard times.

The guilds tried to keep craftsmen from elsewhere out of their towns. But governments often encouraged people who had technical skills to come from abroad.

In this way, many industries spread across Europe.

▲ Many miners were peasants, sent from the fields when there was not much farmwork.

▲ Many people in northern Europe brewed beer. In England a licence was needed to sell it.

▲ Blacksmiths supplied endless local needs, from tools and weapons to horseshoes.

▲ Printers spent a lot of their time producing Bibles and prayer-books.

▲ Carpenters made furniture, and worked with masons and thatchers to construct houses.

▲ Shipwrights designed the galleons which took Europeans across the oceans.

▲ Cloth-weavers often worked outside the town, to escape the control of the guild.

► This beautiful salt-cellar was made by a silversmith in Paris in 1527. The hull of the ship is a nautilus shell.

▲ In the first part of the century, Italian glassmakers were the best in Europe.

▲ Engineers built bridges and helped improve communications between towns.

Glass-making was introduced into England by Venetians. Germans started the clock-making industry in Geneva. Italians developed silk and printing industries in France. Most work of this kind depended on the knowledge of experts, not on complicated machinery. So it seemed only sensible to get hold of the best craftsmen.

▲ Local blacksmiths sometimes also acted as vets, caring for sick animals.

▲ Minters made coins, usually by hand. Minting machines were common by 1550.

▲ A glovemaker. Elizabeth I liked wearing expensive gloves, to show off her long fingers.

New frontiers of knowledge

During the Middle Ages, most scientific knowledge came either from the Greeks or from the Church. Anyone who questioned this 'scientific knowledge' could be burnt as a heretic. But a number of 16th-century men *did* dare to challenge some of the age-old beliefs. 'Knowledge is a great thing,' wrote a brilliant French surgeon, 'but only if it is based on experience.' By carefully observing and experimenting, such men began to form their own scientific ideas.

In 1543, a Polish clergyman called Copernicus suggested that the earth went round the sun. Until then it was taught that the sun went round the earth. In the same year Vesalius, a doctor from the Netherlands, gave the clearest description yet of how the human body worked.

The Church and the old-fashioned universities did their utmost to stop this sort of 'heretical' knowledge from spreading. But they could not stop people being curious. Many intelligent young men, who might have become clergymen in earlier times, were now turning to science instead.

While scientists were busy changing the old ideas, explorers were discovering whole new continents. All this knowledge led a Spanish historian to exclaim in 1552, 'All has now been traversed and all is known.' Little did he know of the frontiers still ahead!

▲ This was one of the first accurate drawings of the moon. It was made by an Italian professor of mathematics, Galileo Galilei (1564–1642). Galileo used the recently-invented telescope to study the night sky. He observed that the moon did not have a smooth surface, but was covered with mountains and craters.

◄ Copernicus thought that the solar system looked like this, with the earth going around the sun, and the moon going around the earth. Uranus, Neptune and Pluto had not yet been discovered. Around the outside are the signs of the Zodiac. Copernicus' writings were not published until the year of his death. Perhaps this was because he feared that the Church would punish him for his 'heretical' ideas.

► This painting shows the laboratory of an Italian alchemist. Alchemists were scientific experimenters who had two main aims. The first was to discover how to make the 'Philosopher's Stone'. This would turn metals into gold. The second aim was to brew a drink called the 'Elixir of Life'. This would make people live forever. The alchemists failed in both quests. Gradually, more modern types of scientist were taking the alchemists' place.

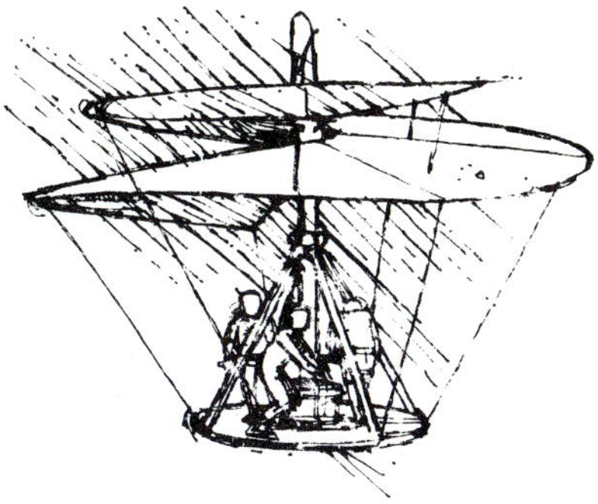

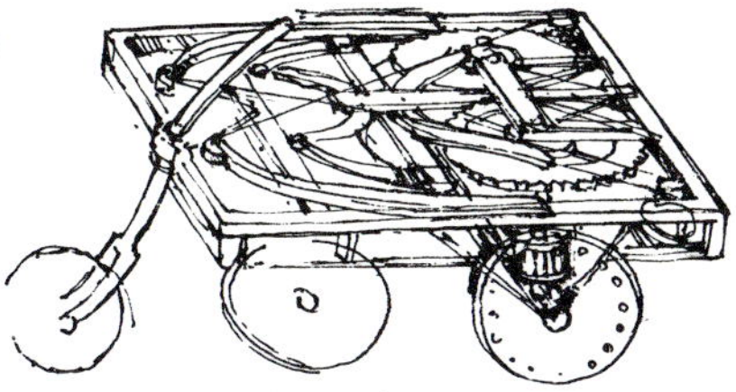

◄ Leonardo da Vinci (1452–1519) was an Italian genius. He designed a flying-machine like a helicopter (far left), and a sort of car (left).

But Leonardo did not know how to power such machines. So they were not built until several centuries later.

◄ This is a drawing from one of Leonardo's notebooks. It shows his idea for an armoured tank. Tanks were not used until World War I, in the early 20th century! The writing below the drawing is very hard to read. This is because Leonardo wrote his notes in code. He wrote from right to left across the page, and turned each letter back to front.

Main events

1485 Henry Tudor defeated Richard III at the Battle of Bosworth. He then became Henry VII, the first of the Tudor monarchs.
1492 Christopher Columbus discovered America.
1494 Charles VIII of France invaded Italy. Start of Italian Wars.
1497–8 Vasco da Gama captained the first sea voyage to India and back.
1509 Henry VII died. His son became King Henry VIII and married Catherine of Aragon.
1515 Francis I became King of France.
1516 Catherine of Aragon gave birth to Princess Mary, who later became Queen Mary I.
1519 Charles Habsburg was elected Holy Roman Emperor. He became Charles V. Hernan Cortes and his men started to conquer the Aztec Empire in Mexico.
1520 Henry VIII and Francis I of France met at the Field of the Cloth of Gold.
1521 Martin Luther was outlawed in the Holy Roman Empire. He went on to set up his own Protestant Church.
1522 Ferdinand Magellan's ship, the *Victoria*, returned safely to Spain after the first-ever voyage right around the world.
1525 Charles V took Francis I prisoner at the Battle of Pavia in Italy.
1527 Charles V's troops ran riot in Rome.
1529 Turks under Suleiman the Magnificent besieged Charles V's city of Vienna, without success.
1531 Francisco Pizarro and his men started to conquer the Inca Empire in Peru.
1533 Without the Pope's permission, Henry VIII divorced Catherine of Aragon and married Anne Boleyn. Anne then gave birth to Princess Elizabeth, who later became Queen Elizabeth I.
1534 Henry VIII replaced the Pope as head of the English Church. England ceased to be a Roman Catholic country.
1536 Henry VIII started closing down the monasteries and seizing their wealth. He also had Anne Boleyn executed and married Jane Seymour.
1537 Jane Seymour gave birth to Prince Edward, who later became Edward VI.
1538 Francis I and Charles V planned to invade England together. Later they argued among themselves and forgot the idea.
1538–9 Bibles in English were placed in all English churches, by order of Henry VIII.
1540 Henry VIII married Anne of Cleves and then Catherine Howard.
1542 Henry VIII had Catherine Howard executed, and married Catherine Parr, his sixth wife.
1545 Members of the Catholic Church met at Trent in Italy. They began to suggest ways in which the Catholic Church could be improved.
1546 War broke out between Charles V and the Protestant Princes in the Empire.
1547 Francis I died. His son became King Henry II of France.
Henry VIII died. Edward VI was still a boy, so his uncle, the Duke of Somerset, ruled for him.
1549 The Earl of Warwick overthrew Somerset. Later he became the Duke of Northumberland and ruled England.
1553 Edward VI died. His half-sister Mary became Queen. She made England a Roman Catholic country again.
1554 Mary married Charles V's son, Philip of Spain.
1555 End of Charles V's war against the Protestant Princes. The Princes and their subjects were given the right to be Protestants.
1556 Charles V retired to a monastery in Spain. He shared out his lands between

Philip II of Spain and Ferdinand, the new Holy Roman Emperor.
1558 The French seized the port of Calais back from the English. Mary died and her half-sister Elizabeth became Queen.
1559 Elizabeth began to turn England into a Protestant country again.
The Italian Wars came to an end.
Henry II died. His three sons ruled France in turn until 1589.
1562 Catholics and Protestants began to fight one another in the French Wars of Religion.
1566 The Netherlanders rebelled against their Spanish rulers. The war went on into the 17th century.
1569 Elizabeth dealt harshly with rebels in the north of England, who wanted the Catholic Mary Queen of Scots on the throne.
1571 The Christian fleet of the Holy League destroyed the Turkish fleet at Lepanto, in the Mediterranean Sea.
1572 French Catholics massacred Protestants on St Bartholomew's Eve.
1580 Francis Drake became the first English sea-captain to sail right round the world.
Philip II added Portugal to his empire.
1587 Elizabeth had Mary Queen of Scots executed.
1588 The English Navy defeated the Spanish Armada sent by Philip II.
1589 Henry Bourbon became King Henry IV of France.
1589 Henry IV ended the French Wars of Religion. French people were now not to be punished for being Protestants.
1603 Elizabeth died. The son of Mary Queen of Scots, King James VI of Scotland, became King James I of England. The line of Tudor monarchs ended, and the line of Stuarts began.

Famous people

Anne Boleyn married Henry VIII of England in 1533. She gave birth to the future Queen Elizabeth I in the same year. Henry had her executed in 1536.

Catherine of Aragon was the daughter of the King and Queen of Spain. She married Henry VIII of England in 1509 and gave birth to the future Queen Mary I in 1516. She was divorced by Henry VIII in 1533.

Charles V became King of Spain in 1516, and Holy Roman Emperor in 1519. He was the most powerful monarch in Europe. He went into retirement in 1556.

Edward VI was the son of Henry VIII and his third wife, Jane Seymour. He became King of England in 1547, but died in 1553 at the age of 15.

Edward Seymour was a powerful noble under Henry VIII. He became Duke of Somerset in 1547, then ruled England in the name of the boy-king Edward VI until 1549.

Elizabeth I was Queen of England from 1558 to 1603, and never married. She was probably the best-loved Tudor monarch.

Ferdinand Magellan was a Portuguese sea-captain. He led the first expedition to sail right round the world, from 1519 to 1522.

Francis Drake was an English 'sea-dog' who led pirate raids on Spanish shipping. He was Vice-Admiral of the English fleet against the Spanish Armada. He became the first Englishman to sail right round the world, from 1577 to 1580.

Francisco Pizarro was a Spanish soldier. He led the tiny army which conquered the vast empire of the Incas in Peru, from 1531 to 1533.

Francis I was King of France from 1515 to 1547. He was a great rival of Charles V. Both wanted to be the most powerful monarch in Europe.

Henry VII was the first member of the Tudor family to rule England, having seized the Crown in battle in 1485. He ran the country efficiently, and died in 1509.

Henry VIII, the son of Henry VII, was King of England from 1509 to 1547. He married six times, and made himself Supreme Head of the English Church, instead of the Pope. He tried to set himself up as a rival to Charles V and Francis I, but had less wealth and power than them.

Hernan Cortes led a small Spanish expedition to Mexico in 1519. By 1521, he had achieved the conquest of the entire Aztec Empire.

John Dudley, a Tudor nobleman, overthrew the Duke of Somerset in 1549, and took control of the government. He made himself Duke of Northumberland in 1551. He was executed by Queen Mary I in 1553, for trying to keep her off the throne.

Leonardo da Vinci was a brilliant Italian artist and inventor. He painted the *Mona Lisa*. He spent much time at the court of Francis I of France, and died in 1519.

Martin Luther was a German professor. He complained bitterly about the corrupt Roman Catholic Church, then set up his own 'Protestant' type of Church. The Lutheran form of worship became popular throughout Germany and Scandinavia. He died in 1546.

Mary I was Queen of England from 1553 to 1558. She made the Pope Head of the English Church again, and had subjects who would not worship in the Roman Catholic way burned to death. She married Philip II of Spain.

Mary Queen of Scots was Queen of Scotland from 1542. She was married to the King of France for a short time, and had a claim to the English throne. She was involved in several Catholic plots against Queen Elizabeth, who therefore had Mary executed in 1587.

Philip II, the son of Charles V, was King of Spain from 1556 to 1598. He was a Catholic, and waged many wars against Protestants and Moslem Turks. He sent the Armada against England in 1588.

Suleiman the Magnificent was Turkish Sultan from 1520 to 1566. His armies conquered and controlled huge areas of eastern Europe, and Turkish advances caused panic throughout Europe.

Thomas More was an adviser and friend of King Henry VIII. He refused to accept Henry as Head of the Church, so was executed in 1535.

Thomas Cromwell was a very hard-working minister of Henry VIII. He organized the break with the Roman Catholic Church and increased the King's wealth. He fell from favour and was executed in 1540.

Walter Raleigh, scholar and adventurer, was a favourite of Queen Elizabeth I. He tried to start English settlements on the east coast of north America.

William Shakespeare was an actor from Stratford-on-Avon and became the best-known playwright in the English language. He died in 1616, at the age of 52.

Glossary

apprentice A boy who was being trained in a craft or skill, for up to seven years.
benefit of clergy The right of clergymen to be tried by their own Church courts.
cardinals Very important members of the Roman Catholic Church. When a Pope died, they met and elected a new one.
colony An area in one part of the world which was controlled by a ruler from another part.
feud A war fought between individuals for personal reasons.
Holy Roman Empire A collection of lands in the middle of Europe. The Holy Roman Emperor was chosen by seven Electors.
heretic The name given to someone who disagreed with the teachings of the Church.
Jesuits The name given to members of the Society of Jesus, started by St Ignatius Loyola. They were Catholics who worked hard to stop the Protestant faith from spreading.
masque A spectacular court entertainment. It included music, dancing and acting.
monopoly A charter which allowed a company or person the sole right to trade with a certain region or in certain goods.
Protestants The name which came to be given to people who complained about the Roman Catholic Church, and set up their own churches.
Roman Catholic Church The only Christian Church in western Europe before the Protestants broke away.
seigneurial dues Payments or services that had to be given to landlords.
spices Pepper, cinnamon, cloves, etc., which came from the East and were used to season food.
tithes Taxes paid to the Church, either in money or in goods.
undergraduate A university student who has not yet taken a degree.

Index

Numbers in bold refer to illustrations